Originally published as *Wow! Ik kan toveren. Magische planten en dieren*
in Belgium and the Netherlands by Clavis Uitgeverij, 2018
English translation from the Dutch by Clavis Publishing Inc., New York

Visit us on the Web at www.clavis-publishing.com.

Wow! I Can Do Magic. Magical Plants and Animals written and illustrated by Mack van Gageldonk
Photos/images: Shutterstock®

ISBN 978-1-60537-635-6

This book was printed in December 2020 at Nikara, M. R. Štefánika 858/25, 963 01 Krupina, Slovakia.

First Edition
10 9 8 7 6 5 4 3 2 1

Magical Plants and Animals

I CAN
DO MAGIC

Mack

Clavis

NEW YORK

Magicians Exist

Do you want to see a real magician? A magician who can make himself invisible, change his shape, or walk on water? Of course, you'd like to meet such a magician! Who wouldn't? Magicians might be closer than you think. Take a close look at these trees. Is there something different about them? No? That's what makes magic so special! You think that nothing is out of the ordinary, but something very special is going on. Maybe all those little green leaves aren't leaves at all. Maybe they're all little animals who changed themselves into leaves, like real magicians . . .

You find a lot of animals and plants in nature who do the same things as a magician. They can make fireworks or light up like a lamp. You don't believe it? That's understandable. Almost no one believes it. Until they read this book . . .

7

I am invisible

I Know a Great Disappearing Act

A **chameleon** is a real magician. Take a close look at him. He looks mysterious, doesn't he? And that's not all. The chameleon can do something wonderful. He can change his colors like a magical ball. He can turn a variety of colors, like purple, or reddish with yellow spots, or patterns of blue with orange stripes . . . You name it!

When you're a color magician like the chameleon, you can use that trick to make yourself invisible. You only have to conjure up the same colors as your background and no one will notice you. That's what the chameleon does. He usually has the same color as the leaves he's hiding behind. The chameleon also uses the color of his skin to show his feelings. When he's calm, he stays green. But when he turns red, you'd better walk away, because then the chameleon is in a bad mood.

I get all the colors of the rainbow

How is it possible that a chameleon can change color? You find the answer in his skin. The cells in the chameleon's skin can change color. They do the so-called "rainbow trick." You see a rainbow when raindrops catch the white light of the sun and divide it into other colors. The **chameleon** does the same. That's magical in itself, but the chameleon can also make all sorts of patterns: here a circle of blue, there a stripe of yellow. The chameleon can actually paint with the colors of the sunlight!

You don't see me

A real magician can make himself invisible. So, you can definitely call a **glass butterfly** a magician! You can guess from his name that he looks as if he's made of glass. At least, his wings do. You look right through them, just like you would look through a window. That's why you don't see him.

And you don't see me at all

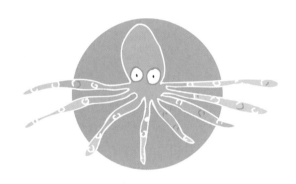

Many magicians live on the land, but you can also find them in seas and oceans. Take for instance the **octopus**. Octopuses know a great disappearing act as well. Not only can they spray a cloud of ink to make themselves invisible, they can also adapt to the colors of their surroundings. The **glass octopus** can even become completely transparent. That makes the octopus one of the biggest magicians in nature and he doesn't even need to use a spell for that!

Chameleons not only change their colors to show you how they feel or to hide themselves. There are more reasons why chameleons practice magic with colors. They choose a lighter color that keeps them cool when it's hot. And when a female is pregnant, she shows it with her colors too. Male chameleons understand that they have to be careful.

I Fly Backward

A **hummingbird** is a magical creature. The little bird can hang very still in the air. He can even fly backward! And also, straight up and straight down, like a little helicopter. The hummingbird flaps his wings so fast you can hardly see it. In the time you take a breath, the hummingbird flapped his wings over a hundred times. When the hummingbird hangs in the sky, he can put his long, thin beak into the heart of a flower. There, deep in the flower, he finds delicious, sweet nectar. The hummingbird uses his beak as a straw to suck up the nectar like a milkshake. And then, he goes to the next flower, and the next. Just like a bee, the hummingbird helps the flowers to reproduce. Flowers are very happy with hummingbirds. So, they keep spoiling the birds with their sweet nectar.

I can shine a light

I Light Up the Entire Forest with My Flashlight

With a little luck, you can see twinkling lights in the middle of a dark forest. These aren't lamps, but **fireflies**. A firefly is also called a "glowworm", but it is neither a worm nor a fly. It's a bug that can fly, that's what makes it confusing. A firefly can light up the bottom of his body. The male firefly often starts to send light signals and waits for a female to flash back. But that depends on the sort of firefly. Sometimes, only the male or the female can light up. Sometimes, the babies can make light too. They use the lights to stay safe from other animals. Enemies are scared of the lights and run off. People don't. To us, these little creatures are magical.

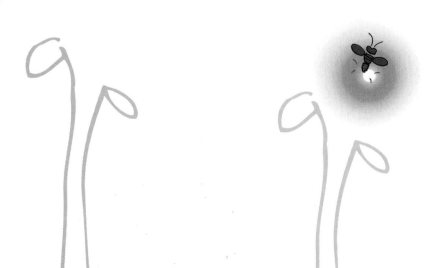

I turn the light on at night

With their long stalks and their beautiful hats, mushrooms look enchanting. There are even magical mushrooms. They glow. These mushrooms grow in Madagascar, an island off the coast of Africa. But you don't have to go that far to see them, because there are also **glowing mushrooms** close to home. These mushrooms probably have a good reason to glow. Scientists think that they do it to lure animals. Animals that touch the mushrooms get spores on their body and help the mushrooms to reproduce.

I illuminate the deep sea

It's completely dark on the bottom of the ocean. There's no sunlight. It's too deep. But even in this darkness, you can sometimes see something flickering. Many fish and **jellyfish** glow. Why would they do that? A jellyfish or fish attracts a smaller fish with the light, to catch it. But the light can also be used to confuse large fish, so the small ones can flee.

I attract fish with light

Sea anemones look like plants, but they're actually carnivorous animals with poisonous tentacles. The **anemone fish** knows how to deal with it, but smaller fish have to be careful. To lure the fish, the anemones do anything to look as attractive as they can. Often, they're brightly colored, and a few species even glow. That looks very pretty, but small fish better stay away.

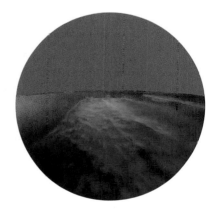

There are big fish in the sea, but also tiny organisms. **Plankton**! A few species of plankton can glow. It's often a blue light, but it can also be white or green. The small plankton is almost never alone. It lives in groups of millions. All together they form big lights that seem to dance on the waves. The plankton illuminates to scare away enemies. When a fish eats it, the fish can glow too.

Me too!

I Celebrate My Thousandth Birthday

Trees can grow very old. A hundred years is old for a human, but it doesn't mean that much to a tree. A tree can easily grow to be two hundred, five hundred, or even a thousand years old. Every year, the trunk of the tree grows a bit bigger and forms a new ring. By counting the rings inside the trunk, you can see the age of a tree.

People think that old trees have magical powers. In Asia, they're even declared sacred. On the Indonesian island Bali are temples next to old trees, where gods are worshipped. The tree that you see here grows there and became so big that you can walk through it, just like walking through a door.

Old trees can be very big and powerful, but there are also old trees that shrunk over the years. There's only a hollow trunk left with a couple of branches and some last brave leaves. At least, that's what you can see. Under the ground, there's more. The roots of a tree can be much older. There are roots in Sweden that are thousands of years old. The tree on top of the roots is just six hundred years old. When it dies, a new tree will grow out of the old roots. There are even older roots found in America with trees on top. The location of these roots remains a secret so no one will disrupt the growth of these magical trees.

We can live to be two hundred years old

Many whales grow as old as humans, about seventy to ninety years. But the **Greenland whale** is an exception. This giant can live to be two hundred years old! In the water are more animals that can grow very old. The beloved **koi carp** with its beautiful colors can easily become a hundred years old; some of them are even over two hundred years old. The oldest koi carp died after its 226th birthday. So, when you see a koi carp in a pond, there's a big chance that he's much older than your grandma or grandpa.

I can live to be 250 years old

Tortoises take it slow and that might be the reason why they live so long. An average tortoise lives to be a hundred. A **giant tortoise** can live even longer. Some walk more than 250 years with that heavy shield on their backs. You'd have to be a magician to keep that up!

I can live a lot longer still

An ordinary mussel doesn't live very long. Thirty to forty years at the most. But not all mussels are the same. In the cold waters underneath the North Pole live mussels that can grow a little older. How about four hundred years! And that's not even the oldest, because the four-hundred-year-old **mussel** has to bow for the record holder that turned 507 years old. No one knows if this is a very special mussel or if there are more old mussels like that.

The **red sea urchin** in the middle can live to be two hundred years old. The plant **Welwitschia mirabilis** grows on the west coast of Africa and can reach the incredible age of two thousand years! But the unrivalled champion is the **Turritopsis nutricula**. This jellyfish can make itself young again. First, it gets older and older, and then, it turns itself into a baby or a toddler again. It's the only species known to man that has this kind of magic. This jellyfish can actually live forever.

Me too!

Me too!

I spy, I spy with my little eye

I Can Still See Everything, Even in the Dark

People hardly ever see him, but he sees you. The **black panther** prefers to hunt in the dark. When it starts to get dark, he opens his eyes wide and pricks up his ears. His eyes are well-developed, and he can see six to eight times better than people in the dark. On the other hand, the black panther sees things less sharp from a distance and he can see less colors. But in the dark, the black panther sees everything. He hides and waits patiently until a deer or rabbit comes close. With a few jumps, he leaps from his hiding place and before the deer knows what's happening, it's caught. After his dinner, the black panther disappears into the jungle again. And no one notices him.

I use the stars as a guide

Many birds can do something incredible. They always know how to find their way home. You might think, that's not so hard, is it? I can do that! Yes, that's true. But can you do it after you were taken to another country, blindfolded? In a country far away, your blindfold is removed, and you have to find your way home without a map or compass. That seems impossible. You know who can do that? **The pigeon**. In a time before e-mail, people used pigeons to take letters to foreign countries. The pigeon finds his way by using the position of the sun and the stars and moon at night. And what if it's cloudy? Then, pigeons can still find their way. They probably use the magnetic field of the earth. How that works exactly is still a mystery.

I can see ultraviolet light

Bees can see something we can't. Ultraviolet light! A rainbow has ultraviolet light next to purple light. But no matter how close you look; we can't see it. So, a **bee** sees a bigger rainbow than we do. Because many flowers reflect ultraviolet light, bees see flowers clearer as well. They can signal to other bees which flowers they have to fly to, to make the best honey.

I can see heat

Snakes don't only hunt during the daytime. Even at night, when it's pitch dark, they know how to find prey. They can do that because they can see heat. **Snakes** see or feel another animal because their body temperature is different from the temperature of the air around it. Because it's dark, the animal doesn't see the snake approaching. It makes most shake with fear, but it's pretty smart of the snake.

Birds of prey have incredibly good eyes too. The **peregrine falcon** is the champion. He looks for small mice by searching the ground with his sharp eyes . Mice better keep very quiet, because the peregrine sees them from miles away!

I Can Hear a Mouse in a Big Pile of Snow

It seems as if they can look straight through you with their big eyes. And they can fly without making a sound. No one hears them. On top of that, they have extremely good hearing. The ears of the **owl** aren't on top of their heads, near the wisps, as you might think. They're more hidden on the sides of their face. When you take a good look at their face, you see it forms a sort of bowl. This bowl can catch the sounds better. That's why they can hear so much more than we can. Try to cup your ear with your hand. Can you hear sounds clearer now? An owl can hear the smallest sound. A snowy owl is the best. Mice, thinking they're safe under a big pile of snow, get noticed by owls. Snow muffles the sound, but it's not enough to escape the owl. He can still hear the mouse, with his magically good ears.

I can hear thunder in a different country

Elephants can hear low sounds that hardly anyone can hear. They can hear sounds like bass, and the roaring thunder, from hundreds of miles away. That's useful when an **elephant** spends days without water, because where there's a thunderstorm, there's rain and water to drink.

I can hear with radar

Bats are every magician's friend. Maybe that's because they can perform a little bit of magic too. They have a sort of radar. When they fly, they make a high-pitched noise. This noise bumps into a tree or a little mosquito and echoes back to the **bat**. He catches the sound with his radar and knows exactly how big the tree or the mosquito is and how far away it is. That's how he can catch the mosquito and why he doesn't bump into the tree.

I can hear even better than bats

What do you do when a bat thinks you're a tasty bite? The bat can easily find you with his radar. In that case, you'd better develop ears that can hear the high-pitched sounds of a bat, so you can run in time! That's what the **greater wax moth** does. It's a sort of butterfly with super ears. The greater wax moth hears no less than one hundred and fifty times better than a human, which makes it the winner for best ears in the animal kingdom.

Whales can talk to each other over a great distance. They produce very low sounds that can reach as far as hundreds and sometimes even thousands of miles. That's how they warn each other where food is, where danger is, and with their songs, they tell when they're in love. The singing of whales can last for days.

I can make poison

I Put a Spell on You

Mushrooms might not look very magical, but be careful . . . they can put a spell on you. Before you know it, you feel like someone else. Most mushrooms are delicious, but don't try to eat all of them. Some are poisonous. So poisonous, that even animals and sometimes people can die from eating them. Be careful with these deadly ones, because they are hard to spot. Some mushrooms make you hallucinate. These are called magic mushrooms. At first, you won't notice it, but then, the mushroom starts to have an effect on your brain and before you know it, you end up in a strange dream. You can be very happy in that dream, but also very sad. You see monsters appear or big spiders in a huge web—all because of such a small mushroom. Mushrooms are real magicians you better not touch.

I can stun you

Look at those pretty poppies. Have you ever seen them in the grass? Or maybe in a little vase? You probably never even imagined these flowers could do something really special. After the plant matures, the flower changes to a sturdy, green boll, which is the roundish pod of the plant. There are seeds in that boll. Poppy seeds, like you find on bread. But the seeds of the **poppy** can also stun you. Morphine is made from poppy seeds. Doctors use morphine to treat pain. When you're in a lot of pain, you won't feel a thing after you've had some morphine. That's how strong it is.

I'm pretty, but poisonous!

These special animals live at the bottom of the sea. They're very pretty **slugs**.
In some countries, like Chile and Alaska, they're eaten. Some say they taste
like big chunks of gum. But it's better not to try this gum. Some species are
poisonous. They won't kill you, but are very dangerous. The species on this
page are very poisonous. You can see that by their colors. When an animal has
the color of its surroundings, there's nothing to worry about. But the brighter the
color, the more dangerous it is. These species seem to use their bright color to warn
other animals to stay away!

You won't survive my teeth

With a length of ten to sixteen feet, the **king cobra** is the biggest venomous
snake in the world. He can kill you with only one bite. And not only you. Even
an enormous elephant won't survive its lethal bite. Still the poison of the
snake is very useful. Little drops of the venom are processed in medicine.
So, the deadly venom can also be used in treatments for some diseases.
This makes the king cobra a big wizard. One who can kill and cure at the
same time.

So, you think that frogs are funny? Not this **poison dart frog**! He lives in the jungle of South America.
He's very brightly-colored and eats poisonous ants. He collects the venom of the ants in his skin.
When you touch the frog, you should wash your hands very well! The poison dart frog is one of the
most venomous animals in the world. A long time ago, Native Americans sometimes used the poison
on their arrows.

I can change myself
into someone else

Me too!

Me too!

I Get Wings

How cool would it be to change into someone else? To look different, to be bigger, or smaller, or to learn that you can fly? Only big wizards can do that. The **caterpillar** is such a wizard. A caterpillar looks common, when you see him walking on a leaf or on a blade of grass. But he's about to do something magical. When the time is right, he withdraws to a quiet place, hanging on a branch or a leaf. And then, it happens. The caterpillar wraps himself in and becomes a pupa. In this pupa, the caterpillar becomes something beautiful. He gets bright colors, long antennas, paws and . . . wings. Such a transformation is called a metamorphosis. The caterpillar becomes a butterfly. Any caterpillar can do it. Incredible, isn't it?

I Rise Out of the Water

Dragonflies are one of the most beautiful animals. They fly like little helicopters over the water. They were once born and raised in that water. After the little egg came out, the larva immediately dived into the water. The **dragonfly** is then a brown creature. It already has the shape of a dragonfly, but it looks more like a worm. But then, it happens. The larva peels underwater. And again. And again. Sometimes ten or fifteen times in a row. And there's always a bigger larva coming out of the old skin. Eventually, the dragonfly larva crawls out of the water. It's big and strong now, and ready to transform one last time on a leaf.

I can be all shapes and colors

The imitation octopus lives among the corals in Indonesia and Australia. It can both change its shape and its color. The **imitation octopus** can transform into fifteen other animals, like a snake, a flatfish, or a walking piece of coral, in a second.

I become someone else

Ladybirds can also turn into someone else. They start their lives as a little caterpillar. This caterpillar changes into an orange-brown pupa, hanging on a leaf. Suddenly, the pupa opens up, and the caterpillar is now a little bug! At first, the bug has a yellow-green shield. But this changes into red or another color, and the bug even gets dots before it's a real **ladybug**.

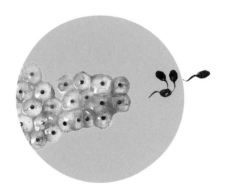  

Frogs have a metamorphosis too. First, the mother lays hundreds of eggs called frogspawn. Out of the eggs come little pollywogs. And then starts the big change. The pollywog changes piece by piece. It gets a little snout, bigger eyes, a thicker tale, and four paws. A bit later, the animal crawls out of the water—as a grownup frog. This frog lays eggs, and the big trick happens again.

I'm a doctor

If you're sick, you may need medicine to get well. A **chimpanzee** knows that. If he has a stomachache or muscular pain, he knows exactly which medicine he should take. However, a chimpanzee can't see a doctor for a pill. They're doctors themselves! Lots of plants grow in the jungle, and in those plants are substances that can cure. Lime leaves are good to keep mosquitoes away, the leaves of the Aspilia plant help against stomachache, and carbonized wood gets toxins out of the intestines. When another anthropoid, the **orangutan**, has babies, they're carried by the mother. That's quite heavy. The mother orangutan knows that she has to eat the leaves of the Vernonia plant to ease her muscular pain. Chimpanzees and orangutans are like real medical doctors.

I make fireworks

The bombardier beetle is like a tank. When an ant attacks him, the **bombardier beetle** shoots hot gasses from the back of his body to the attacker. These gasses explode. The beetle bombs the ant. To prevent the gasses from exploding in his own body, the beetle keeps two substances in separate spaces under his shield. The substances come together when the beetle blows them out. That's when they explode.

I become a giant

If a blowfish is threatened, he has an impressive answer. He blows himself up to a large, thorny ball by sucking up water. The **blowfish** has a rubbery skin, which stretches completely. As soon as the enemy has fled, the blowfish pulls back its spines, spits out the swallowed water, and then swims as a slim fish. He only does his magic trick when he's in danger.

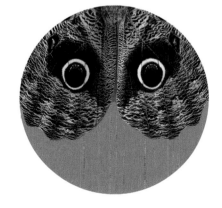

Wisdom is better than strength, they say. Many butterflies are more than smart. On the back of their wings, they have two large, dark spots. From a distance, these spots look like the eyes of an owl. Almost every animal is a bit scared of the big, strong owl. And they're also afraid of the big dark spots on the wings of the butterfly, though this little creature isn't big and strong. Have you already figured out the name of this magical butterfly? It's an **owl butterfly**.

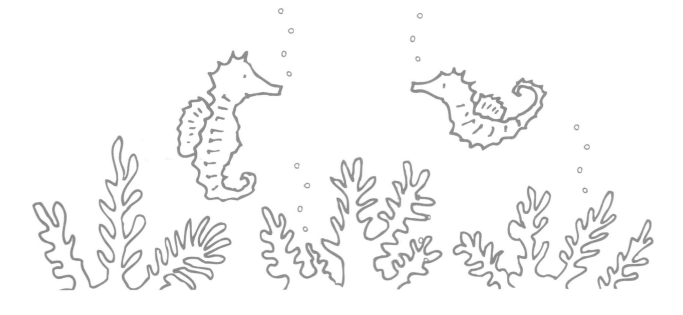

Do You Believe It Now?

So, do you believe it now? Wizards do exist! Now you know where to find them: in nature. And there's even more magic! **Seahorses** turn all the colors of the rainbow when they're looking for a partner and they don't even need to say a spell to do it. Even unicorns exist! Sea creatures called **narwhals** have horns up to three feet long—a true unicorn of the sea! Scientists have different theories about the horns. They could measure the salt content in the water or be used to impress their girlfriend. Nobody knows exactly what it's for. Is that bad? Oh no. That makes the narwhal a magical animal. You can't understand everything—certainly not a wizard!

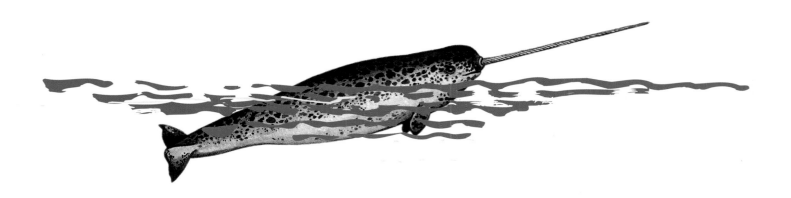

Index